The Bathroom Was My Dungeon

THE BATHROOM WAS MY DUNGEON
True Tales of Surviving an Abusive Marriage

Angela R. Edwards

Foreword By:
Dr. Marilyn E. Porter

www.Redemptions-Story.com

Redemption's Story Publishing, LLC, Houston, Texas (USA)

The Bathroom Was My Dungeon

The Bathroom Was My Dungeon:
True Tales of Surviving an Abusive Marriage

Copyright © 2020
Angela R. Edwards

All Rights Reserved.
No portion of this publication may be reproduced, stored in an electronic system, or transmitted in any form or by any means (electronic, mechanical, photocopy, recording, or otherwise) without written permission from the publisher. Brief quotations may be used in literary reviews.

Print ISBN 13: 978-1-947445-77-2
Digital ISBN 13: 978-1-947445-78-9
Library of Congress Control Number: 2019955523

Some names and identifying details have been changed to protect the privacy of individuals.

Scripture references are used with permission from Zondervan via Biblegateway.com.
Public Domain.

For information and bulk ordering, contact:
Redemption's Story Publishing, LLC
Angela Edwards, CEO
P.O. Box 62287
Houston, TX 77205
RedeemedByHim@Redemptions-Story.com

Angela R. Edwards

Dedication

In Loving Memory
of my father and protector,
James W. Boyce, Jr.

Thank you, Daddy, for dutifully fulfilling your role in my life by being a model gentleman and showing me how a **REAL MAN** should treat your daughter.

Thank you for saving me.

Acknowledgments

First and foremost, always giving honor and glory to the **Holy Trinity: God the Father, God the Son, and God the Holy Spirit.** Without Him, I would not be here today to bear witness of His goodness and how His hand of protection on my life saved me time and again from certain death.

To my very empathetic, loving, and understanding husband, **James M. Edwards:** Thank you for your help in reminding me that there are truly *GOOD* men in this world. I love you beyond mere words!

To my children, **Anequilla L. Foots** and **Gerald Savage, III:** Although you were unaware of the abuse I endured, I thank you for continuing to love me unconditionally. Your patience and understanding during that trying time in my life do not go unnoticed. I love you both to the moon and back!

To my ever-supportive mother, **Marlowe R. Scott:** You have never ceased to amaze me. I thank you for allowing me to live my life and make my [many] mistakes. I not only learned from **them**, I gleaned valuable lessons from **YOU** along this life's journey—even when you thought I wasn't paying attention. I love you with an everlasting love!

To my BFF [and Foreword writer], **Marilyn E. Porter:** I don't know how you did it, but you walked this walk with me and kept me encouraged along the way. The strength you possess is remarkable and needed in this wicked world. Keep on living and breaking down those barriers that prevent others from being blocked from their blessings! You did it for me, and I know you will do it for them. Blessings today and always! I love you, Murl!

To my brothers, **Carl E. Reid** and **James D. Boyce:** I must laugh as I say this, but… Thank you for teaching your baby sister how to fight and defend herself! I would've never guessed the need would arise to go to battle the way in which I did. I love you both, my "Big Brohams"!

Lastly, I acknowledge my abuser's *purpose* in my life. Although he was the reason behind why this book was able to be written, it does not go without saying that my testimony of survival — **despite his best efforts to see otherwise** — will help another be set **FREE** or, better yet, altogether *AVOID* the trauma associated with abuse.

Prologue

With the onset of the #MeToo Movement, more and more people have taken to pen and paper to share their horrific stories in print form of abuse in **MANY** forms. For me, countless not-so-famous individuals have been given a "voice" to their survivor stories long before it became "the thing to do." Through the Battle-Scar Free Movement and associated *God Says I am Battle-Scar Free* International Best-Selling book series, women, men, and teens have sown healing words into the lives of others for quite some time now — all while embarking on their own healing journey. It wasn't easy for many of them, but they penned their way to restoration. They have taken a stand, refused to remain a victim, and, with a collective shout, said, *"LOOK AT ME! I'VE BEEN ABUSED...BUT I'M STILL HERE!"*

The Bathroom Was My Dungeon is a product of my personal abuse testimony dating back to my mid-twenties (at the time of this writing, I will soon celebrate being alive for half a century). It was critical to my mental wellbeing that I released those things that have been hidden away because of shame, regret, disappointment, and bitterness. Plus, **GOD** told me it was time. No other reason matters more than listening and adhering to His voice. This book was written with you—the reader—in mind, though. The transparency of the stories contained herein was necessary to ensure **YOU** grasp the intensity of living a life of confusion with a person commonly known as a "functioning addict."

I must forewarn you: There are no holds barred. Although this literary piece is not laden with curse words, they are present because that is how I expressed myself at that moment. I apologize in advance if you are offended in any way by the use of foul language. This book is for adults only, so it is my prayer that you will simply *FEEL* the situations, embrace and then quickly release my pain, and hastily overlook my former faults in all their humanness.

Today, I am no longer the tragically victimized woman you will read about in this book. I am a **SURVIVOR** and **THRIVER**—terms that may be familiar to many (if not *ALL*) of you! I do not take credit for the recovery I have undergone. Instead, I give **ALL** glory, honor, and praise to my Heavenly Father for His hand of protection over my life as I went through the fire. It was during that time—when I was faced with life or death at the hands of my abuser—that I humbly returned to my Christian roots and memorized Psalm 91 in its entirety. I share it here with you and pray you have your own uplifting passage(s) of God's Holy Word stored away in your heart for those times when you need to be emboldened during difficult times on your life's journey.

Angela R. Edwards

Psalm 91 (KJV)

"He that dwelleth in the secret place of the Most High shall abide under the shadow of the Almighty. I will say of the LORD, He is my refuge and my fortress: my God; in Him will I trust. Surely, He shall deliver thee from the snare of the fowler, and from the noisome pestilence. He shall cover thee with His feathers, and under His wings shalt thou trust: His truth shall be thy shield and buckler. Thou shalt not be afraid for the terror by night; nor for the arrow that flieth by day; nor for the pestilence that walketh in darkness; nor for the destruction that wasteth at noonday. A thousand shall fall at thy side, and ten thousand at thy right hand; but it shall not come nigh thee. Only with thine eyes shalt thou behold and see the reward of the wicked. Because thou hast made the LORD, which is my refuge, even the Most High, thy habitation; there shall no evil befall thee, neither shall any plague come nigh thy dwelling. For He shall give His angels charge over thee, to keep thee in all thy ways. They shall bear thee up in their hands, lest thou dash thy foot against a stone. Thou shalt tread upon the lion and the adder: the young lion and the dragon shalt thou trample under feet. Because He hath set His love upon me, therefore will I deliver Him: I will set Him on high, because He hath known my name. He shall call upon me, and I will answer Him: I will be with Him in trouble; I will deliver Him and honour Him. With long life will I satisfy and shew Him my salvation."

Amen and Amen.

Foreword

Full of youth and vigor. Full of love and laughter. Full of trust and tenacity. Although naivete took center stage, the presence of God was always there—as was I...the friend, the confidant, the partner in an attempt to "adult" at the highest level. There was very little real wisdom to govern the attempt. I wonder what the adults in our lives would have done if they had only known a smidgen of the secrets that settled between us.

Infidelity.

Abortions.

And, in the case of my dear Sister-Friend of more than 40 years, some of the most unthinkable abuses one could imagine.

Demonic is the only word I can gather in my mind.

Unlike most of the free world, I have been patiently awaiting the arrival of this book. I have supportively watched and served my dear Sister-Friend as she went about the business of assisting **OTHERS** in telling their stories—building books with pages that serve as hospitals for the domestically abused. If you are reading this book, then you have likely read at least one of the titles in the Battle-Scar Free Movement book series. Thus, you know that recovery, restoration, and the spirit of resilience lies in those pages.

I assure you of this one thing: This completion of Angela's journey into the dark world of "what goes on behind closed doors" will bring you to your place of healing. I could not be prouder at this very moment as I pen these words, simply because it is time to map out her journey back to life, love, and laughter—as only **MY** friend can tell it.

I remember this time in our lives so keenly, as though it had just happened a few months ago. I remember the *smell* of this dude and how it reminded me very much of what I had known as a child growing up in the most drug-laced part of our small city. I remember thinking how much *different* she was than what I saw in his eyes. I remember thinking how *kind* and *gentle* of a soul Angela is, and, if anyone could love the broken man I saw standing before me back to wholeness, it would indeed be her!

And so, I proceeded to do my job as a friend. I loved and supported her every effort to be with the man she loved.

Long before we began to jump on the narcissism bandwagon (these days, everyone who even so much as loves themselves just a little is considered a narcissist), the signs were there that she had encountered a person who needed to have life woven around his needs.

As young women, we don't see that as a mental dysfunction. No. We see a man who loves us *SOOOO* much, he just wants to consume all his days getting to know us.

WRONG!

In this case, just as it is with many others, what is happening is "they" are getting to know your weaknesses so that they can pounce on and demolish you at your lowest.

Thus, there were many moments I was not aware of during this time of complete and utter foolishness (abusers are **ALWAYS** foolish; the very act of abusing someone is foolish) and shame (the victim of the abuser *almost always* feels shame). However, I was always very well aware that **something** about my friend was different—as if the light had gone out in her eyes. Even as I was enduring my own 20-something struggles, I never took the time to ask direct questions. Still, there was a "knowing" I could never shake.

I have grown up in the midst of abusive, addicted, manipulative, disrespectful males **AND** the women who loved them. I knew what it looked like when I would bump into my Sister-Friend at the local Acme supermarket or have a random phone call. I knew the *SOUND* of an abused woman. I knew the *ENERGY* it took to hide and protect the abuser from accountability. Notwithstanding, I believed in the idea of "love conquering all." I had faith that if anyone—and I do mean **ANYONE** in the world—could love that broken, little man back to wholeness, it would be Angela.

The streets talk (or should I say the **PEOPLE** in the streets talk). I heard things from time to time and dismissed most of it as jealousy…'cause let me tell you: Angela had a body to kill! I was sure some of the talk was just women being jealous and hateful, so I would simply make it known that she was my homegirl and… Well, let's just say I was a force to be reckoned with in my day, and once I made my affiliation known, I never heard another word. Even then, there were some mentions of the man and a few sightings that made me nervous. By that time, I was on my way to total surrender to Jesus, so I began to pray and trust God for a suitable end to the madness.

I will end my trip down "Memory Lane" right here.

The Bathroom Was My Dungeon

TODAY, I want to introduce you to this woman—this **NEW** woman. Still my old friend, but a **NEW** woman. This woman didn't allow the depths of disrespect, discounting, and devaluing to stop her from loving, living, and laughing.

This woman—still my old friend, but a **NEW** woman who rose defiantly in the face of an abuser who had a death wish for her.

This woman—still my old friend, but a **NEW** woman who did the work to get the healing she needed to raise her children alone, find love again, continue to honor her parents, remain a trusted confidant, *AND* build a powerful business that freely gives voice to those who often cannot or are afraid to speak out for themselves.

This woman—this **NEW** woman but still my old friend who thinks it not robbery to share the intimate details of her very own journey, in order that another might be compelled to get out of the grips of domestic violence themselves.

I am honored to sit in the space of having known, having seen, and having watched her become better, stronger, wiser, greater, and more powerful than just about any other woman I know personally.

Angela R. Edwards

Mrs. Angela R. Edwards is my old friend and sister. It would be remiss of me not to give honor to the man who came along to show her that love does not leave bruises: Mr. James Edwards. I love you both.

~ Dr. Marilyn E. Porter, BFF ~

[Best Friend Forever]

www.marilyneporter.com

The Bathroom Was My Dungeon

"The Meeting"

To understand the depths of my story, one must first know the history. Although it has been almost a quarter of a century since the events that led to the writing of this book, the memories continue to invade the recesses of my mind from time to time. To that end, I will do my best to be as transparent as my recollection will allow.

It must first be noted here that the portion of my life's story that follows dates to when I broke up with my child's father. Events of my life that happened before then do not necessarily "matter," so I will not bore you with those details. The juicy stuff came by way of the **choices** I made and have since taken full responsibility for them.

For the sake of storytelling, I will call my now-ex-husband "Kase." I think that name is appropriate and definitely fitting because there were far too many times during our brief marriage when I thought I would *"catch a case."*

At the time Kase and I met, the relationship with my child's father was nearing its end. The natural progression of our union was not leading us to the altar (after being together for three years), and marriage was what I wanted. After tiring of being denied my selfish "want," I found myself vulnerable and, well, needy.

Enter in Kase.

I was leaving for lunch one day from the insurance broker's office where I was employed, and Kase was walking through the parking lot. We crossed each other's paths and exchanged pleasantries.

Him: *"Hello!"*

Me: *"Hi!"*

I kept walking to my car, ready to enjoy my hour-long lunch at home.

Him: *"Where are you going so fast?"*

Me: *"To lunch! I only have an hour."*

Him: *"What's your name?"*

Me [thinking]: *"Uh-oh. This is not good. He is far too handsome to simply brush him off!"*

The Bathroom Was My Dungeon

Me [speaking]: *"Renay."* I remember giving him a fake name because I didn't expect ever to see him again. No harm, no foul—right? That was until…

Him: *"Hi, Renay! I'm Kase. I live right over there."* I followed the direction of his pointing finger and noted that he lived in the house that shared the parking lot with the business in which I worked.

In a panic, I chose to quickly end the conversation with the atypical, *"Nice to meet you, Kase, but I must go – **NOW**."* I jumped into my car, sped off, and, when I peeked in the rearview mirror, saw that he stood in place and watched me drive away (the reverse will be significant later in my story.) I went home and, during my quiet time, thought long and hard about that chance encounter with the handsome stranger. He had piqued my interest.

Was it really that **OR** was it that I was ready and willing to take a ride on the wild side?

Little did I know, it was the latter that would shape my year-and-a-half-long story of perpetual abuse in various forms at the hands of the one I "loved."

Angela R. Edwards

*I tell my story...
not for the glory,
but so that others may know
HOPE.*

The Bathroom Was My Dungeon

Table of Contents

DEDICATION	VI
ACKNOWLEDGMENTS	VII
PROLOGUE	IX
PSALM 91 (KJV)	XII
FOREWORD	XIII
"THE MEETING"	XIX
"ROSES AND CONFUSION"	1
"LOVE'S CLEANSING POWER"	7
"SEX FOR A FIX"	12
"WEDDING BELLS WERE RINGING"	15
"FRIENDS APLENTY"	20
"THE WHITE MEAT PUNCH"	24
"BOYS, BOYS, BOYS"	30
BABY MAMA BRINGS THE DRAMA	30
SOUTHERN BOUND	32
"THE FAMILY'S ROOTS GO DEEP…NOT!"	37
"GOING NUCLEAR"	43
"THE DRAGON'S DUNGEON"	46
"THE LAST LOOK"	52
"MY DADDY DEAREST"	57
"GONE UP THE RIVER"	60

"BROKEN GLASS"	61
"THE GAVEL ENDED IT ALL"	64
"THE LESSON"	66
"TODAY, I AM BATTLE-SCAR FREE!"	69
PEN YOUR PAIN: THE HEALING BEGINS	75
ABOUT THE AUTHOR	83
CONTACT THE PUBLISHER	87

The Bathroom Was My Dungeon

"Roses and Confusion"

The day I met Kase is one that is hard to forget. He left quite the impression on me that wowed a woman who was, in essence, yearning for attention and excitement.

And so, my story begins…

When I returned to work after my lunch break that day, I was saddened not to see Kase anywhere around. Yes, I confess: I drove slowly through the parking lot while eyeballing his house to see if I could catch sight of him. He was nowhere to be found. I entered the building, sat at my desk, and drummed up a conversation with the other ladies in the office about the "handsome stranger in the parking lot." In that discussion, I asked if either of them had ever seen him (that, of course, required that I provide details of just how handsome he was). Neither of my coworkers had any idea to whom I referred. For some odd reason, that made me feel special. After all, he could have just as easily encountered either of them in the parking lot, just as I did—but I was the 'chosen one'!

The workday continued as usual. Calls were answered. Appointments were made. Documents were typed. Meetings were held. There's nothing extraordinary about the day to write about here — except for the fact that every few minutes, I would casually stroll to the window to see if I could catch a glimpse of Kase either in the lot or anywhere near his house. Each survey of the scene was met with disappointment. It was almost as if he didn't exist! *Had I brushed him off too hurriedly? Did I appear overly disinterested? Would I **EVER** see him again?*

That evening, at 5:00 p.m. sharp, I got off work, walked downstairs, and made my way to my car. As I approached, I immediately noticed something was resting on the front windshield. From a distance, I couldn't make out what it was. Whatever it was had taken up a considerable breadth of the glass front. I approached with caution, only to be surprised by a dozen long-stemmed red roses wrapped in purple cellophane with a card attached. ***Talk about confusion!***

Immediately, thoughts of who it could be from went to my child's father. He and I weren't on the best of terms, so it was natural first to think he was trying to make up by showering me with a gift he had **NEVER** bought for me before. I grabbed the roses, opened the car door, climbed inside, and proceeded to open the card. I wasn't ready for the message that awaited me:

The Bathroom Was My Dungeon

"WILL YOU HAVE DINNER WITH ME? KASE"

He included his number on the card. I do believe I sat in place for approximately 15 minutes or more in a state of shock. Since I didn't take the time to share with Kase that I was "otherwise involved," I didn't know what to make of his romantic gesture that was coupled with a boldness I hadn't experienced in years.

I couldn't take the roses home, so I ran back inside my job before my boss could lock up for the night and placed them on my desk. I knew their presence would create quite the buzz in the morning, so I braced myself for the onslaught of questions that were sure to be asked by my colleagues.

Moving along…

That night, I thought about Kase. I knew I was wrong as two left feet as I laid in the bed next to my child's father while thinking about another man, but I couldn't help myself. My thoughts were all over the place.

Should I?

Could I?

What if?

How?

Where?

When?

The questions kept coming, with no clear answers at the ready for any of them.

The following morning, I awoke and readied for my day as usual. I was in a much happier place, which I am **SURE** mystified my significant other. After sending everyone in my household off to the start of their day, I made my way into work. I was hoping I would see Kase, but it was not meant to be. Just as I expected, when I arrived and entered my workplace, my coworkers were ready and waiting. I must mention here that I noticed the roses had been moved from where I placed them, leaving me to know they had taken a peek at the card. *People sure are nosy, aren't they?*

The discussion that day leading up to our lunch hour was **ALL** about Kase. The ladies in the office knew my current "situation," so they offered both advice *AND* asked a slew of questions as they came to mind. I assured them I had taken all aspects of Kase's proposal into consideration but had yet to make up my mind. I was undecided and knew that when noon came, I would be forced to make a decision once and for all because Kase would be waiting for a reply. Although I had his telephone number, I shied away from calling him. I was not ready for **THAT** conversation yet.

Just as I suspected, when lunchtime came, Kase was waiting for me by my car. The conversation was very flirty, leaving me to feel like a teenage girl who was spoken to by her childhood crush for the first time. We soon settled into a very comfortable dialogue and decided to have lunch at a local restaurant that was within walking distance. During that time together, we chatted with ease. His personality was on full display, and I countered with allowing mine to shine through as well. It was an hour that "sealed the deal." The vulnerable state I was in had opened the door to full-blown puppy love. Although I had shared with him that I was in a relationship, I suppose it was the latter part that he grabbed hold of and ran with:

"The relationship is close to ending."

The next few weeks included a whirlwind of secretive phone calls (this was before Caller ID came on the scene) and my getting out of the house just to see him for a few minutes here and there. He didn't seem to mind that he was in a position of playing "second" to another man. Slowly but surely, Kase's love grip sank its way into my heart. After deciding I could no longer play the game, I told my child's father the truth: I was seeing someone else.

The break-up was brutal. He was blindsided and hurt by my admission. He acted the way virtually anyone would respond when they have been deceived. He left our home, but not quietly. He was distraught (as I would have been were the situation reversed) and came out of character. In all the years we were together, the anger and passion he displayed on the way out the door were things I never even knew he had in him! Nonetheless, our relationship was officially over. It was time for me to move on.

I was so selfish—and there would be a hefty price to pay for the pain I caused him.

The Bathroom Was My Dungeon

"Love's Cleansing Power"

There's an adage regarding relationships that states something along the lines of, *"Don't open that door until the other one is closed."* I should have taken heed to that advice.

Almost immediately after the break-up with my child's father, Kase and I started spending every free moment together. If my children and I weren't at his house, he was at mine. We shopped together, went to the park as a family, and even had weekly "Movie Night," which often included choices made by my children (I had another child by another man before my second child's father and I met). In hindsight, I should have taken notice that he was obsessive. When I say, "Every free moment," I mean **EVERY** free moment. I think I overlooked the obvious because I was "in love."

Guilty as charged.

After about three months of us living apart and maintaining separate residences, I suggested that he move in with me (moving in with him wasn't an option because he resided in a one-bedroom apartment, and I had two children under my care). Much to my surprise, he denied my request!

He stated that because his apartment was state-funded, he couldn't easily break the lease. I had no choice but to understand and accept that as his truth, but I came to learn his reason wasn't that simple…or 100% true.

To give a little backstory without being overbearing, Kase was a convicted felon on parole. That significant fact was not told to me until long after we had started getting deeply involved. Would it have made a difference in how I felt and fell for him? I will never know. Due to that aspect of his life being hidden from me (who thinks to ask, *"Are you a convicted felon?"*), my love for him had already taken hold and wasn't letting go. (Be mindful that this was a **LONG** time ago, and the instant nature of the internet and background searches were not options.) So, when he said he **COULDN'T** move in with me, I believed him. He did, however, give me a key to his apartment—with the agreement that I would **NEVER** come over without letting him know I was on the way.

Well…

Allow me to preface what I am to say next with the following: I am one who follows the rules. I believe they are in place for a reason and, more often than not, will follow them to the letter. When a mutual agreement is added, I'm all in! Those rules will **NOT** be broken.

There are exceptions to every rule.

The time came when I tried calling him all day, and he wouldn't answer or return any of my calls. After much frustration and worry set in, I grabbed his apartment key and drove to his apartment—about a five-minute trip. When I arrived, his apartment was pitch black. No lights. Not even a flicker of the television glowing through the blinds. Nothing but total darkness. At that moment, a sense of dread overtook me, but I couldn't turn away. I **HAD** to know Kase was okay on the other side of that door!

I approached, placed the key in the lock, turned the knob, and entered. I was **NOT** prepared for what I saw before me. My "love" was there…laid out on the couch…**and high out of his mind!** He was totally oblivious to my presence. I turned on the light, walked over to him, then had a seat on the chair facing the opposite of him. It was then I understood why he wasn't responding to me.

On the coffee table that stood between us was a crack pipe, lighter, and tiny bag with nothing but drug residue inside.

I recall attempting to wake up Kase, but he wouldn't budge. *Just how high was he?!* He was still breathing, so I knew he was alive. His unresponsiveness scared me, so I ran into the kitchen, filled up the largest cup I could find with cold water and ice cubes, and threw it directly into his face. The water mixed with the sweat that had beaded up on his forehead, and he managed to come out of his drug-induced stupor long enough to be startled by my sudden appearance. He then seemed to pass out again. As I stood over him filled with anger and disgust, he mustered up two words:

"I'm sorry."

I then grabbed the crack pipe and threw it at him. I was appalled and couldn't believe I didn't see that revelation coming from a mile away. How could I, you might ask? He frequented the part of town where the drugs were sold. He did, however, have family in the area, so I never would've put two-and-two together had I not cold-busted him. I honestly cannot remember the entirety of the conversation that followed, but I do know it consisted of him asking for forgiveness…and me forgiving him.

Love is a strange thing. The things we tolerate and accept when love shows up on the scene tend to be bizarre and unexplainable. That was me. I refused to see the new circumstance for what it truly was, so I simply accepted that he was an addict. I was young and naïve, too. I just **KNEW** I could *"LOVE HIM CLEAN"!* I have since learned that doing so is a virtual impossibility. An addict must want the change for himself or herself first before transformation can begin to take place.

Once Kase's dirty, little secret was exposed, that set our relationship on a new path—one which I wasn't at all truly familiar with.

Angela R. Edwards

"Sex for a Fix"

Among the list of things I came to learn about Kase was that he knew many of the people I associated with. You see, he was a popular deejay in the area. He used to host parties and spin the turntables at them. For a time, he also starred on an FM radio station that played R&B and Hip-Hop. I will be among the first to say he was very good at his craft. I used to watch and listen in amazement as he practiced blending music to perfection. When he tried to teach me, I was a horrible student. Although I have rhythm and can keep up with the best of them, it takes a particular skillset to mix sounds and have them merge flawlessly. I left the deejaying to him.

Being mindful that I stated we knew many of the same people (to include my neighbors), most of them were well aware that he was an addict. In the same breath, they couldn't understand our being together and assumed I, too, was addicted to crack cocaine. That was **FAR** from the case. With all honesty, I can say I have *NEVER* even **tried** the drug—but it's said that "birds of a feather flock together," so I had to settle with those things thought about me and simply live my truth: I was in *LOVE* with an addict.

The Bathroom Was My Dungeon

My family would be shocked to know that once I accepted Kase's addiction, I used to make runs to that seedy part of town I mentioned previously to purchase crack for him so that he would "feel better." What do I mean? Addicts of various types go through severe withdrawal when they do not have anything to fulfill their body's needs. For Kase, his attitude was a serious problem when he was "coming down off his high." He was as different as night and day when he was high and when he wasn't. I was faced with either a gentle giant or an evil tyrant, and it all depended on how stoned he was at any given moment. I obviously wasn't thinking clearly, as every trip made could've landed me in jail. After all, I was a mother who had everything to lose! How many times did I make that trip? Too many times to count.

I am truly grateful for God's protection. It was no one **BUT GOD** who kept me safe. My guardian angels were certainly working overtime—of that I am sure.

There was one time I made "that trip" to get Kase a quick fix that is more memorable than any other. He had called in advance and told the dealer I was on the way. When I arrived at the designated spot, the man approached my car, leaned into my lowered window, and asked, *"So, are you ready to do this?"*

"**DO WHAT?**" I asked. Never before had I **ever** done more than a speedy pick-up and drive off.

"Your dude said you were going to sex me down for this bag." He reached into his pocket and pulled out a small bag with the crack rock inside, dangling it in front of my face.

Instantly, I was terrified beyond measure. I put the car into drive and, as I drove away, screamed, *"I'M NOT DOING A DAMN THING WITH YOU FOR THAT SHIT!"*

When I returned to Kase empty-handed, he was furious! He had already received the call from the dealer, letting him know I didn't fulfill my end of the deal they made. No sex; no drug! In no way was Kase angrier than I! **He tried to pimp me out for a bag of crack!** He and I said horrible things to one another that day, after which we broke up and went our separate ways…for all of three days.

I should have walked away and never looked back right then, but my heart still yearned for him. We made up and, in an instant, all was well. He again apologized and promised never to subject me to something like *that* ever again. He never did. Sadly, however, that is not the end of my story.

"Wedding Bells Were Ringing"

As time progressed, life with Kase settled into a routine that I believed I could not be freed from. The path I chose (remember...we all have choices) was one filled with toxicity and pain—one I came to embrace as my new normal because of the heartache I had caused my child's father. Some would call it 'karma.' As for me, I felt **cursed** with having to live life as I came to know it because it was my punishment for the irrational decisions I made and continued to make.

Roughly five months into our tumultuous relationship, Kase and I started talking about marriage. That discussion happened, of course, when he wasn't high. When he was in his right mind, our conversations were entertaining and meaningful. Such was the case when nuptials were mentioned. After enduring verbal and emotional abuse of varying degrees, my self-esteem was all but void. I honestly believed his narcissistic speak when he said, *"We might as well get married. No one else is going to want you after this!"* That was my official proposal. There was no ring nor him romantically getting down on one knee to ask for my hand in marriage. Awful, I know.

Getting married seemed the logical thing to do at the time, so we began planning for the big day.

It must be noted here that he wasn't working a steady job, so all the financial responsibilities fell on me. I maintained my job, paid the bills, bought the food, provided for my children, and did **ALL** the things a *man* should do as the provider. He, on the other hand, would work a job just long enough to earn that first paycheck, cash it, and then disappear to get high for days on end until every penny was spent. Only then would he return home with his apologies—just to do it all again in a week's time or less.

So, as you can see, the pattern he established was one I came to accept. With or without him, my life had to go on. All the while, I was stressed out. I had lost weight (likely looking like the addict others had come to believe I was). My hair was falling out, leaving me to choose to purchase wigs to cover up the hair loss (in my mind, I told myself I was making fashion statements with my different "looks" to justify the critical state of "being" I was in). My patience with my children was razor-thin. Through and through, I was suffering something horrible.

It was the path I chose. I had to walk the walk.

The Bathroom Was My Dungeon

The wedding planning began. I insisted on getting married in my home church, and the pastor refused to perform the ceremony without pre-marital counseling. **THAT** was interesting. We were scheduled for six sessions before the service could take place, but time and again, something would happen, and we couldn't go as expected. Sometimes, it was "our fault"; other times, the pastor had to reschedule. It was a mess! We managed to squeeze in two meager 30-minute counseling sessions before our wedding day, which was a mere six months into our relationship. Neither of us was truly ready for such a commitment, but we forged ahead nonetheless.

As for what to wear on our big day, **THAT** was a near disaster. We didn't have the money to have the ceremony I desired, so Kase borrowed a cream-colored suit from his cousin, and I was given a white skirt suit from my best friend. Fortunately, she and I were the same size. Otherwise, I have **NO** idea what I would've worn. (The two of us still laugh about the moment I approached her in a panic.) There was no pure white, long-flowing gown like that of many little girls' dreams.

While trying to keep the ceremony as formal as humanly possible, we asked our closest friends to be in the wedding party. My father was our "driver" that day. He chauffeured us around in his black Lincoln Continental. What a guy! My mother skillfully made my veil and all the floral arrangements, to include the men's boutonnières and the women's corsages. They were burgundy and white—and beautiful! She really did her thing to make sure my special day was the best it could be.

The wedding itself went off without a hitch. We were on time, there were roughly 25 people in attendance scattered throughout the church, and before we knew it, we were "Mr. and Mrs."

The reception was held at a local bar where Kase deejayed. The mere thought of an official honeymoon was fleeting at best. All in all, I spent about $200.00 on the wedding, with the biggest expense being the two-tier cake. Everything that *wasn't* paid for was gifted to us (i.e., the reception was a gift from the bar's owner). I'm grateful for the small things that and the people who made our day so special, although I do believe many came because they couldn't **believe** we were getting married and had to see it happen for themselves.

All that love I had to give and the lifetime commitment I made to Kase hadn't changed a thing. In fact, my circumstances were only going to get progressively worse from that day forward.

The Bathroom Was My Dungeon

An odd fact that I cannot fail to mention here is that the bar where the reception was held was later sold and converted to a **FUNERAL HOME!**

I'll just let that sit right there as you work to grasp the significance…

Angela R. Edwards

"Friends Aplenty"

Once Kase and I were married, he reported to the parole board that he and I were going to live together and that he was finally going to relinquish his government-subsidized housing. They readily agreed to the new arrangement.

If I thought life before marriage was testy (to say it mildly), life after was about to go up another notch.

Now, I cannot and will not sit here and bash my ex to no end. As stated previously, I fully accept responsibility for the roles I played and will admit my faults.

To begin, I instilled a lack of trust in him because I was basically two-timing when he and I first got together. There's that expression so commonly said by both women and men that comes to mind:

"Once a cheater, always a cheater."

That is not my **TRUTH**. I have an appreciation for commitment but found myself in a weakened state when Kase and I first met. That's no **excuse**, but that's my *"why."* Trust me when I say that men had tried to approach me many times before Kase came into the picture; however, I was committed to my child's father and never gave those others a second glance.

Anyway, as I said, the lack of trust began to make its appearance literally one week after our wedding day. That following Saturday, I was accused of sleeping with his friend — the same man who stood as the Best Man in our wedding! There are a few things wrong with his accusation:

1. His friend was **MARRIED**.

2. I wasn't physically attracted to him **AT ALL**.

3. I was **NEVER** alone with him.

So, from where did Kase's suspicion come? Prepare for a wild ride!

Remember I said Kase and I knew a lot of the same people? Well, one of the people we had in common was a girl I went to school with. She and I remained friends after graduation, and she would come to my house often. That was nothing new. She was in my life and visited me long before Kase's entry. I came to learn that my friend and the friend I was accused of having sex with were actually the ones having an extramarital relationship (we live in such a small world, don't we?). Once that was revealed, both of them would sometimes come to my house to "meet up." They used my spare bedroom for their little love nest from time to time, which caused a sense of unease with Kase. There was no one in the **WORLD** who could tell him I was *NOT* the one spending time alone with his friend…**not even his friend!** Kase was convinced dude and I were doing "the nasty" every chance we had.

It was during one of his rants that Kase dropped another bomb on me:

Before he and I met, **MY** friend (the one I went to school with) and he used to have sex **OFTEN**.

What was I to do with that information? Do you mean to tell me that neither one of them **NEVERRRRR** thought to mention that little tidbit *BEFORE* we married? *Really?* That admission caused me to pause at that moment. I recall being stunned to silence. Our argument came to an abrupt end that day. I needed to hear **HER** say it.

Well, when confronted, she didn't deny it. She went on to explain that she was very happy for me, hoped he would settle down once and for all, and blah, blah, blah. In all honesty, I didn't know what to expect from **MYSELF** as to how I was going to react to her admission. Surprisingly, I thanked her for sparing me from the truth. Otherwise, I likely wouldn't have married Kase.

Love is blind! *OH, HOW I NOW WISH SHE HAD TOLD ME EARLIER!!!*

So, I was dealt a bad hand. I was left with no choice but to look past "the past" and move forward with my "husband." Meanwhile, the accusations continued—even after I stopped the naughty couple from coming to my home to sex it up. If I wasn't being accused of sleeping with his friend, I was charged with being a whore with the entire town.

I'll tell you: When things were good, they were fabulous! When they were bad, they were truly **HORRID!**

Roughly a month into our marriage, the verbal and emotional abuse was not enough for him. The **TRUE** Kase made his appearance.

Angela R. Edwards

"The White Meat Punch"

As is common with victims of abuse—*no matter the form*—we are often ashamed and make excuses for the abuser. Notice, I said, **"WE."** I'm culpable. I did just that for Kase.

Physical abuse entered our union one day when I had gotten fed up with his constant disappearing after stealing money out of my wallet to run off and get high. On that dreadful day, he grabbed the car keys (after going into my purse) and went out the door. I was **SO** done with his antics by then and followed behind him while screaming, *"If you take my car, I'm going to call the police!"*

WHY DID I SAY THAT?

With his fingers on the handle of the car door, he stopped, turned to look at me, and said between clenched teeth, *"I told you to **NEVER** call the cops on me!"* (He did tell me that a long time ago. He told me **never** to threaten his freedom.)

In the blink of an eye, he rushed toward me with his right fist raised and then **BAM!** He punched me in my face! I fell to the ground, dazed and confused. He stood over me, screaming only God knows what (I cannot recall because my ears were ringing from the blow). Next thing I knew, he came at me again with his hands in a position to choke me while I was down. Instinctively, I lifted my right leg and kicked him in his penis. That action stopped him long enough for me to get up off the ground.

Once I stood (shaking but standing), I noticed blood droplets falling on my all-white outfit. **THAT** pissed me off more than the hit! While he was still bent over and nursing the pain in his groin, I gave him a right-handed uppercut, sending him stumbling backward. He looked up at me in disbelief. He couldn't believe I hit him — and neither could I! I knew right then that we were about to get into an all-out fight in the backyard.

I had assumed wrong.

In response, he picked up the keys he had dropped when I kicked him, and then wobbled his way back to the car, holding himself the entire way. What happened next **still** shocks me to this day, even as I write my story.

When I realized he was going to drive off with my car anyway, instead of stopping to call the police as I had threatened to do, I jumped into the backseat and slammed the door shut. I told him, *"You are **NOT** taking my car anywhere without me in it."*

"So be it," came his reply.

Let me pause here. You may be wondering, *"Where were her children during all of that?"* Thankfully, they were spending the weekend at their grandmother's house.

Kase started the car, backed out of the driveway, and began making his way to whatever his destination was to be. I remained in the backseat, crying and tending to the open wound that seemed to have an endless supply of blood. We rode in silence (other than an occasional sniffle from me). Roughly five minutes into the trip, he made a sudden turn onto a back road I never knew existed. I thought to myself, *"He's going to kill me and leave me back here! No one will **EVER** find me!"* I began to quickly think of the words I could say to save my life.

"I'm sorry. You know I would have never called the police. I was just mad. I love you!" **Yes. Those words should save me. I'll say that to calm the beast.**

Once he finally came to a stop, I noticed we were at the edge of a rushing river. I thought, *"Please, Lord! Don't let him throw me in there!* **I CAN'T SWIM!**" We sat in silence for a few minutes more before he finally got out of the car. When he came around to my side of the car and opened the door, he reached in to grab me to help me get out. He wasn't rough at all. I had braced myself for the fight of my life, but Kase was gentle as a lamb. He wrapped his arms around me and, for the first time since we'd known each other, cried a deep, sorrowful cry. Between his tears, his apologies were boundless. He then guided me to sit in the front seat and closely observed the damage he had done to my face. There was so much love in his touch. Somewhere in there was the man I fell in love with not so long ago.

Kase took notice that my favorite white outfit was ruined from the blood and dirt from our little tussle, and he promised to replace it. I found that to be significant to mention because that was the closest to an acknowledgment I would receive that he had done something terribly wrong to me.

I took a look in the passenger-side mirror to see the damage for myself. I was shocked by what I saw. A massive lump had formed just over my left eye—and I could **SEE** the white meat, meaning his bare fist had cut my head wide open...deeply. I should have had him take me to the hospital, but we both knew how **THAT** would have turned out for him.

I should have gotten stitches (that's how **DEEP** the wound was). I was left with a permanent battle-scar that I wear to this day. I don't try to disguise it, either. It's a part of me and a constant reminder of where I've been.

After some time, he drove back home, carried me (literally) into the house, laid me on the couch, and tended to my wound as best he knew how. A sprinkle of peroxide, a lot of pressure to stop the bleeding, and an oversized band-aid made it all better. Oh! I can't forget that he followed that up with a kiss to my "little boo-boo." Although I remained in a state of shock, I quickly forgave him and promised never to bring it up the events of the day ever again.

The fun part was figuring out how to explain to anyone who asked what happened to my head.

"What happened to you?"

"Why the knot?"

*"Why the **BIG** band-aid?"*

Immediately, I began to compose my best lie. I'm not really good at it, but I had to cover up for my man's violence (an atypical victim's move)!

The Bathroom Was My Dungeon

Without fail, the first person to take notice and ask about the noticeable boo-boo was my mother. With a straight face, I told her I had dropped the iron and, when I went to retrieve it, scraped my head on the edge of the ironing board. See? I **TOLD** you I wasn't good at lying! She gave me the side-eye — indicating she did *NOT* believe me whatsoever — and told me to be more careful. Convinced that I had gotten one over on her, that was the same lie I told anyone who asked.

Looking back, I must laugh at my stupidity. My mother had afforded me the opportunity to be honest, and I chose not to walk through that door. **What was I thinking?! Who does that?** I'll tell you who: victims of abuse who are in denial.

Angela R. Edwards

"Boys, Boys, Boys"

Unfortunately, I wasn't the only victim of Kase's "recreational" activities. It seems as if he left a trail of destruction everywhere he went. The following two instances are most memorable for me because, at the time, I thought I was the **ONLY** one being victimized by him.

Baby Mama Brings the Drama

Kase was quite the baby-making machine. He had seven children by five different women. The children were scattered up and down the East coast of the United States. Two of the seven resided in the same state as us. Not long after we got together, I was introduced to two of his boys. They were amazingly adorable, friendly, and favored their father to the letter. Paternity could **NEVER** be denied by Kase, as they were the spitting image of him (I cannot say the same for a few of the others, but that's not my concern any longer—although I do recall when I questioned him repeatedly about "them," he screamed, *"I'M THEIR FATHER! NOW, DROP IT!"*). Defensive much, Kase? I never mentioned it again.

Anyway, the mother of the two boys and I got along as best we could for the sake of their sons. We were cordial but didn't spend much time in each other's presence. Our lengthiest exchange in person had to be all of five minutes — and that was the day we met so that she could 'see' who her sons were going to be around. I respected that about her.

She called the house one day when Kase wasn't home, and it somehow turned into a 30-minute Q&A period. Primarily hosted by her, I could tell she was emotionally scarred and needed someone to talk to *(where were her friends?).* As it turned out, she and Kase weren't together as a family because he was abusive to her as well. Our stories regarding him were eerily similar, but I would only divulge those things that were (for lack of better words) "common knowledge." Some of the highlights of the conversation were:

- ➢ Kase liked to punch on women.

- ➢ Kase knew how to string his words together to demean and beat a woman down, oftentimes worse than his fists.

- ➢ Kase wasn't a model father (no shit, Sherlock).

- ➢ Kase's addiction was more essential to him than anything or anyone on the planet.

Early on, I couldn't understand why she chose **ME** to discuss **MY** man/**HER** "babies' daddy." While on the phone, she shed genuine tears and, by the end of the call, was *begging* me to leave him…before it was too late. Needless to say, I didn't listen to her. In my need to be defiant, I thought she was trying to be slick by coaxing me to leave him so that she could have her family back together. The enemy got me **GOOD** with that destructive self-chatter!

I never told Kase about that call. I'm almost sure she didn't, either. I imagine that if she had, I would've gotten a good tongue-lashing **AND** beatdown for discussing him with **HER** (of all people). I kept close to my chest all that she and I had discussed. My understanding of Kase's true character had been heightened, but I *still* wasn't discouraged enough to leave him. I was so naïve!

Southern Bound

So, I believe it's safe to say that Kase was a weapon of mass destruction. Those he managed to affect with his lackadaisical lifestyle were likely scarred for life. Did he care? I believe the answer is a definitive and resounding **NO!** Had he possessed one iota of concern, the people who loved him wouldn't have been hurt time and again.

The Bathroom Was My Dungeon

I recall the time Kase and I made a trip down South to pick up his oldest son to spend one month of the Summer with us. We had borrowed his cousin's van to make the eight-hour trip (yes, that is eight hours **ONE WAY**). By the time we arrived, it was nearing nighttime, and Kase was lost. We had to repeatedly pull over to phone booths along the way to find our way to the house. (This was long before cell phones were commonplace.) Eventually, we arrived, rested for about an hour, and made the return trip home. By the time we walked through the door, daylight had come, and I was downright exhausted.

After settling his son in for his stay, I went to my room for a short nap. Kase and his boy left to take the van back to his cousin after asking me to pick them up when I awoke. I agreed, and before I knew it, was knocked **OUT!**

When I finally stirred and climbed out of bed, I got myself together and drove to his cousin's house. I quickly took notice that everyone was outside hanging around on the front lawn…but where was Kase? I parked, got out of the car, and approached his son. I asked where his father was, and he said, *"I don't know. He dropped me off and kept going with the van."* An immediate feeling of dread overcame me. I then asked his cousin, *"Where's Kase?"* His reply was similar to the son's—except **HE** said it with rage.

I told his son to get in the car with me. We went home and waited for Kase to either call or come back. We waited…and waited…and waited for **DAYS**. In his absence, I did my best to entertain a teenager while still caring for my own young children. We went to the mall, the basketball court, and the movies.

No Kase.

No call.

NOTHING.

Meanwhile, his cousin was phoning me constantly. *"Is he there? When's the last time you heard from him?* **WHERE IS HE WITH MY VAN?"** I understood his frustration but had no new information to offer him.

No, he wasn't home.

I hadn't heard from him since he left to drop off the van.

His guess was as good as mine when it came to knowing where Kase was with his van.

The Bathroom Was My Dungeon

After five days had gone by, I made up my mind that I was **NOT** going to "babysit" his son while he was out gallivanting only God knew where. I called his son's mother and explained that I needed to bring him home but that I was not in a position to make the eight-hour drive alone. I asked her to meet me halfway, which she did.

As we made our way down the highway, his son and I talked about how he felt regarding his father's absence. He was such a mature, young man. He stated he was not at all surprised and that it was not the first time Kase left after committing to spending quality time with him. He did, however, amaze me when he said, *"But this will be the **LAST** time he will do this to me!"* How brave of him! **HOW BOLD!** I knew he meant every word (although he might not have had the power he felt at that moment to buck up against the adults in his life). Still, I had to applaud him for his bravado!

You know how people often apologize to another when someone else has done something wrong? I did just that. When we finally met up with his mother, I gave his son a hug before parting ways and spoke my sincerest of apologies for his father's absence. What I **DIDN'T** say was, *"See you again soon!"* **THAT** would have been an outright lie. The welcome mat had been folded up—not because of anything he did, but because his father was **NOT** going to place the burden of responsibility on me for his wrongdoing again. I sometimes wonder: When was the last time they saw each other after that?

Strangely enough, Kase wasn't at all upset that his son was gone after returning home **EIGHT DAYS** later. I suppose I dodged a bullet that time.

"The Family's Roots Go Deep... Not!"

Another facet of this story that is significant is a relationship Kase had with a woman who was his "cousin." It seemed that almost everyone we knew was related to him somehow! With his mother and father having divorced long ago, his family ties extended far beyond anything I was used to.

I think of Oprah Winfrey here.

"YOU GET A COUSIN! YOU GET A COUSIN! AND YOU GET A COUSIN! EVERYONE GETS A COUSIN! HOORAY!"

Moving along...

The cousin I am referring to here was another frequent visitor. For reasons unknown to me at the time, she didn't like me. The **LAST** thing I thought was that she was jealous of our marriage. After all, **THEY WERE COUSINS**, right? **WRONG!**

One day, I went to retrieve the mail out of the mailbox, and there was an envelope inside with no stamp and no return address. That made it obvious the envelope did not go through normal postal service channels. It had my name on it with just the street address. Strange, I know. As I made my way back inside, I opened the envelope to find a five-page handwritten letter that was penned on yellow legal paper. I thought, *"Who in the world took the time to do all of that writing when they could've called?"* I quickly went to the last page to see who signed the letter. Nothing. No name. No fancy autograph.

Once inside, I separated the mail, settled down in the living room, and started to read the letter. The long story short version is that the writer stated she and Kase had been having sex for years before we met and continued to do so whenever he visited her, even after we married. As I read, I looked for some indication of who the mystery woman was but could not pinpoint anyone in particular. It was highly infuriating! She went on to say she was in love with him and that **SHE** should have been the one walking down the aisle to marry him. I was thrown for a loop! **Who on God's green Earth did Kase and I have in common that would say such a thing?**

After experiencing firsthand the propensity for Kase to become enraged at the drop of a hat, I decided to hide the letter until I could determine the source. It didn't take long at all for the mystery woman to come forward.

The Bathroom Was My Dungeon

Are you prepared for another outrageous adventure? ***Ready or not, here we go!***

It was late in the afternoon when I heard an unexpected knock at my door. *"Who could that be?"* I thought. **EVERYONE** knew not to come to my house unannounced. When I opened the door, there stood "cousin." I greeted her and explained that Kase wasn't home. As I was talking, the person who drove her there suddenly took off. I thought that was strange in itself because, as I said, Kase wasn't home. There was no need for her to be alone with **ME**. We didn't even care for each other "like that"! She asked if she could come in, stating that there was something we needed to discuss. With a slight hesitation, I invited her in.

Just as she got comfortable, a feeling of trepidation overcame me. The hairs on the back of my neck and arms stood on end, letting me know whatever she was about to say was **NOT** good—and I wasn't wrong. The conversation that followed went something like this (as best I can recall):

Her: *"Did you receive the letter I put in your mailbox the other day?"*

Me [with a lifted eyebrow]: ***"THAT WAS FROM YOU?!"***

Her: *"Yes. I'm sorry, but I had to tell you because I know he never would."*

Me [eyebrow still raised]: *"BUT YOU'RE HIS COUSIN! WHO DOES THAT?!"*

Her: *"We're not blood cousins. We were raised together, so we CALL each other cousin."*

Me [both eyebrows raised]: *"BITCH! YOU GOTTA GO! GET YOUR FUCKING LYING ASS OUT OF MY HOUSE!"*

Her: *"I don't have a ride. I'll just wait until Kase gets back. He'll tell you."* She sat back, crossed her legs, and got comfortable.

It must be noted here that she was calm and confident. Not once did she raise her voice during the conversation. I was the one freaking out!

Me [lifted brows now replaced with a look that could kill]: *"THE HELL YOU WILL! I'LL GIVE YOU A RIDE. LET'S GO!"*

If you could have seen the smug look on her face as she picked up her purse, you likely would've wanted to cut her throat like I wanted to at that moment. She was proud and self-assured. She just *KNEW* she had won her man! She had gotten the rise out of me that she expected. (I kicked myself **HARD** for that response, by the way. I'm usually much more level-headed than that, but what was "usual" about what was revealed?!)

I grabbed my keys and shoved her out the door. She easily weighed twice as much as me, but I handled her like a fluffy stuffed animal. Once in the car, I turned to her and asked, *"Are you happy now?"*

With a smile from ear to ear, she replied, *"Yep!"*

THAT did it! I had something ready for her ass!

I calmly began the drive to her house. About midway, I pulled the car over to the side of the road, told her to get out, and to walk the rest of the way. She looked at me like I was plum-loco. To understand her concern, I must share here that I had pulled over on a back road that was lined with nothing but blueberry fields on both sides for **MILES** — and it was getting dark. She said, *"I am **NOT** getting out of this car. You **WILL** take me **ALL** the way home."* Her demand fell on deaf ears. I then turned on the hazard lights, put the car in park, reached underneath my seat, and pulled out the mini steel baseball bat I kept there ever since Kase tried to pimp me out for his drugs.

In the confines of the front seat, I drew back the bat as far as I could and said to her, *"I will **NOT** repeat myself."* She must've seen the look of impending death I had in my eyes because that smug look she had maintained instantly vanished. She quickly removed her seatbelt, gathered her purse, and fumbled with the handle to get the door open. No sooner than her left foot touched the ground, I put the car in drive and peeled out of there, purposefully kicking up dirt and gravel at her in the process. My little four-cylinder car put in some **WORK** that day!

Being honest, that was not my *finest* moment in life, but it is high on the list of the most ***gratifying***!

As I drove away, I allowed the force of the wind to shut the passenger's side door. I didn't care what happened to her. Let the wolves eat her alive. **I. DID. NOT. CARE.** I was *DONE* with the shenanigans and playing "nice." I couldn't **wait** to confront Kase with the letter and news about her pop-up visit.

You may not be surprised to know that she got to him before I could…

The Bathroom Was My Dungeon

"Going Nuclear"

As I drove home after "cousin's" swift exit from my car, I was filled with a mix of emotions that were difficult to manage. I had a new 'shotgun rider' that came in the form of anger, confusion, distrust, disgust, and fear all balled into one. Oh! I can't forget to mention that **JOY** was riding along, as well. **JOY** was what enabled me to make it safely back home. **JOY** was what I felt behind taking a stand and doing something totally out of character for once since being with Kase—no matter the consequence.

I arrived home and waited patiently for Kase's return. On that day, I knew he would return soon, as he was actually out making a quick run to the store for me. Our relationship and his mental state were in a good place, so I had no doubt he would be back soon enough—and he didn't disappoint.

What I *DIDN'T* expect was for him to come into the house **ANGRY**. My attitude was already at 200% and, when adding his 200%, we were at 1,000% without delay! He had the nerve to come in **ENRAGED**! I was flustered by his brashness. ***Why was HE angry?***

I liken what he must have felt like to how one might feel after being backed into a corner and must determine how to get out of the predicament unharmed. When pleading one's case doesn't work, anger may step up and handle its business. I believed he already knew our situation was in critical distress. Immediately, I knew he had spoken with "cousin" before coming home, releasing me from the opportunity to blindside him with my newfound information.

Whatever nuclear explosion you can imagine is precisely what occurred when Kase and I began our quarrel. By the time he arrived, I had the five-page letter spread out on the couch — a letter I now know he knew about before me. During our "little spat," he told me he had asked "cousin" not to write that letter. The bitch didn't listen. I also learned (from his version of the story) that **MOST** of what she said was accurate: they were sex partners for a long time *(Ewwww!)*, but only **BEFORE** we got together, and no, they were not blood family. How was I to believe they were not still sleeping together when the lies and deceit from him were perpetual?

That day, he and I fought like two guys. I mean, we *REALLY* threw down! At any time, if I felt he was getting the upper hand, I would find something within reach to throw at or hit him with. Everything was fair game. A lamp. My high-heel shoe. The stereo speaker. A feather duster. (LOL!) We were at **WAR**, and I refused to lose! Our two-person brawl ended when we were both bloodied and exhausted. There was no one to referee our fight, so it had to end one way or another.

I'm grateful to be here still to tell you my story.

After calming down enough to talk civilly, Kase somehow managed to convince me that it was her jealousy and attempt to destroy our marriage that prompted "cousin" to act out. I kept asking him, *"Why? What did I ever do to her?"* He assured me she was just crazy and obsessive. He even joked, *"You love this dick, too!"* as he grabbed himself. That was the icebreaker that was needed at that exact moment. We laughed and laughed…

With the snap of the fingers, we were, indeed, back in our proper place as the loving husband and wife. Life was good for a short while after that day. I was satisfied (although only temporarily) with his response to the neurotic lady's outcry for attention and love from **MY** husband.

Ohhhhh, but that addiction beast was loitering in the background, waiting to pounce yet again in the biggest way possible. **IT'S SHOWTIME!**

"The Dragon's Dungeon"

Things between Kase and I had calmed considerably since the "cousin" incident—much to HER chagrin. He and I pinky-swore that he would not allow himself to fall victim to her tomfoolery by giving her any leeway or "hope" that they would be together. That meant Kase would need to spend quality time with me, assuring me that he was genuinely disinterested in her. I felt victorious! I had beaten the bitch!

That feeling of accomplishment was only temporary, though. Kase's spirit of addiction needed to be fed again, and he was an all-too-willing participant in the enemy's scheme.

One night, Kase was getting high in the house. By this time, since the cat was out of the bag, he would sometimes choose to participate in his illicit activity at home. What more was there to hide, right? He would either lock himself away in the downstairs bathroom or our upstairs bedroom until he got his fix. I no longer fought with him over his addiction. **THAT** was a losing battle—one I no longer had the energy to combat. On that night, things felt eerily different. I cannot put it into words. "Different" is the best I can come up with at this time.

The Bathroom Was My Dungeon

While he was getting high in the bathroom, I was on the phone with a friend. As I walked through the house chatting away, I made a pitstop at the bathroom door just to listen to be sure he was still alive in there. When I heard the flicker of the lighter, I knew all was well. It must be noted here that when I stopped at the door, I also ceased from talking and asked my friend to be quiet for just a moment. As I walked away from the door, I resumed my conversation. Shortly after, I heard the bathroom door open, indicating that he was done with his dirty deed, so I ended the call.

As he turned the corner to enter the living room, he was sweaty from head to toe, and a horrid odor emanated from his body through his clothing. For those who do not know, crack cocaine prompts a flood of sweat to pour off an individual's body due to the sudden increase in their heart rate. The smell that permeates from their body is the effect of the chemicals from the drug finding their way out through their pores and sweat. It's never a pretty scene.

Along with the sweat and odor, Kase's eyes were glassy and bugged out. He stumbled his way over to me as I sat on the couch, leaned over (while holding onto the arm of the sofa to steady himself), and asked, *"Why did you call the cops on me?"*

I was **BAFFLED**! *"I didn't call the cops on you! What are you talking about?"*

He leaned in closer. *"I heard you on the phone. You told them I was in the bathroom getting high!"* **(OH, MY GOODNESS! THAT SMELL!!!)**

"I was talking to my friend, Kase. What reason would I have to call the cops? You getting high in the bathroom is nothing new!" Again, the hairs on my neck and arms rose. Something seriously wrong was about to happen.

Suddenly, he grabbed me by the arm and forcibly dragged me into the bathroom (I still have the scar on my right arm from him digging his nails into me). He quickly slammed the door, turned the lock, and pushed me down onto the toilet. **"LET. ME. OUT. OF. HERE. KASE."** I spoke each word very pointedly as I looked him square in the eyes. He was in another world that was far, far away. He didn't hear me.

I was **NOT** prepared for what happened next.

I took notice he had not cleaned up his "mess." The crack pipe, lighter, and a small piece of the cream-colored crack rock in a bag sat on the edge of the sink. As he stood blocking the door, he reached and grabbed his drug paraphernalia. After breaking off a small piece of what remained of the rock, he placed it into his pipe and tried to hand it to me.

"What do you want me to do with that?" I screamed.

*"I heard you on the phone. You called the police. Since they're on the way, you and I **both** should be high when they get here."*

Had that fool lost what was left of his MIND? He MUST have!

*"I'm not putting that thing in my mouth, Kase! I am **NOT** getting high with you!"*

He kept pushing it toward me; I kept pushing it away. That game went on silently for a few minutes. I absolutely **REFUSED** to give the enemy that entrance into my life. I've seen what it did to Kase and many others. I saw the devastation left behind in the lives of families. I bore witness to the inability to afford keeping the demon fed, causing addicts to "do things for things." I wanted no direct part of that life. I was already in too deep as it was by accepting his lifestyle.

He kept pushing; I kept denying.

When he got tired of our little game, he picked me up and threw me into the bathtub. Another thing that must be mentioned is that when crack addicts are at the peak of their high, *some* seem to gain remarkable physical strength…if only for a moment. It was at that peak when he picked me up with ease and tossed me like a rag doll. I landed in the tub with a thud and a bang to the back of my head. Instantly, I was dazed. I likely suffered a concussion, now that I think about it. I rubbed the sore spot and looked up at him, pleading with my eyes to be let out of the bathroom.

He grabbed the pipe and lighter again and yelled, *"YOU WILL HIT THIS!"*

I hollered back, *"NOOOOOOO, I WILL NOT!"*

He then climbed into the tub with me and squatted on my legs. I was trapped. I literally felt as if I were in a dungeon with no way of escape. The tower's fiery dragon had me locked behind closed doors with a heavy chain, waiting to seal my doom. What could I do? The beast was spewing out balls of white-hot fire!

As crazy as this may sound, I was **glad** I was able to hold off long enough for Kase's need to get his next fix. Up until that moment, I had only seen people smoke crack in the movies. I used to think they were exaggerating for the sake of a good show, but I was mistaken.

Kase remained in the tub with me, put the pipe to his mouth, lit the opposite end with the rock, and inhaled deeply. The crackling sound from the chemicals reacting to the fire is a sound I will likely never forget. The way his body responded to that hit is also something I will always remember. He leaned his head back, allowed the drug to take effect, and then exhaled. At that moment, his body relaxed enough for me to wiggle my way out of the tub. He was totally oblivious to my frantic exit.

He stayed in his self-made dungeon for about another 30 minutes or so. He must have forgotten all about him having me locked in there with him because when he finally exited, he was as calm as still waters on a windless day.

I chose to never mention that incident to him. There was no argument, no harsh words spoken. After all, if he could quickly forget, so could I! I was the classic victim of abuse — but I was a fighter and a survivor!

Angela R. Edwards

"The Last Look"

As life would have it, our marriage continued to have its highs and lows. After the dungeon incident, I was on a close guard. I realized that the enemy of my soul—Satan—was on the warpath. He wanted me subjected to his will and his way, and he was trying to use the one I loved to draw me into a life of outright **HELL**. I wanted no part of it, so my spiritual (and often physical) fight continued.

I dealt with the whispers behind my back from those who said, *"Look at her. I know she's getting high with him."* One of my neighbors, who was also an addict, once approached me and asked if I had any crack I could sell her! It was really crazy out there! There was no need trying to defend my honor with her because she and countless others just **KNEW** I had fallen prey to the enemy's tactics. In response to her question, I simply stated, *"No. I do not."*

Time progressed, and my marriage had *almost* made it to the one-year mark before it all came to a roaring head.

After hanging out with a couple of friends one night, I returned home and found my husband entertaining company. He was seated in the living room with a man I had never seen before. It was very late at night—around midnight—and I was tired, so I began to make my way upstairs to prepare for bed. I didn't even **CARE** who the guy was; I just wanted sleep. About midway up the stairs, Kase called out to me and said, *"He needs a ride home. I can't drive because I'm high. Can you take him?"*

I looked up at the top of the stairs and then back at Kase. I was just feet away from my bedroom. My bed was calling my name. I let out an exasperated sigh and said, *"I can drive, but I'm not going with him alone. You have to come, too."*

The three of us climbed into the car, and off we went. What neither of them told me was that the man lived 45 minutes away! The ride was pin-drop quiet, except for the times when the man gave directions to his destination. We made it safely there, dropped him off, and headed back home.

Roughly 15 minutes into our return trip, Kase's high began to wear off. Out of nowhere, he started an argument with me, stating that he didn't like the way I disrespectfully spoke to him in the presence of his friend. Personally, I did not find what I said disrespectful. With a hint of sarcasm in my voice, I went on to explain: *"I thought you would have appreciated my concern about not wanting to be alone with a stranger."* That did it! I had talked back to him when he was sober and clear-headed—and he was **MAD!**

That night, the roads were slick from a recent rain event. At the time the argument started, we were traveling down a long, dark road that had cornfields on both sides. As the argument grew more and more heated, so did Kase's anger. Suddenly, he reached across, grabbed the steering wheel, and jerked it out of my hands. That made the car veer off the road and into the cornfield on the **opposite** side. Imagine for just a moment: We were traveling at **50 miles per hour** when he snatched the wheel. The car slid across the road with ease due to the moisture on the surface. We went violently sailing into the cornfield some 50 yards or more before coming to a stop. I sat in the driver's seat in a state of total numbness.

What in the hell? Did this man just try to kill both of us?!

A few seconds later, reality set in. We had to get out of the field before someone came snooping. I skillfully backed out and made it back to the road. I took one last look at the path the car had made and silently apologized to the owner. He was sure to be in for a surprise the next time he visited his field!

The Bathroom Was My Dungeon

I had no words for Kase. When I glanced over at him, I saw that he had a look of panic on his face *(go figure)*. Up ahead, there was a tiny corner store that was closed for the night. I pulled into the parking lot, parked as close as I could get to the lone light, jumped out of the car, and surveyed the damage. Corn stalks and ears were entangled in the front and rear bumpers. Shredded shoots lined the bottom of all four doors and the wheel wells. The poor car had been through something! It looked like a light blue scarecrow! Kase remained in the car while I did my walkaround.

I walked back to the open driver's side door and said to him, *"I'm not going anywhere else with you. Get out."*

"I'm not going getting out. Get back in this car! Let's go home!" he demanded.

"You have lost your damn mind, Kase! You tried to kill us! GET. OUT." I knew at that moment I had reached my end. The marriage was **OVER**. He, however, didn't budge. I then saw a phone booth and began walking toward it. I was going to call 911 and report the "accident." He must have seen the phone, too, and knew my intent. There was no turning back.

I continued to make my way to the booth when I heard not one, but **TWO** car doors shut. I turned to see him sitting in the driver's seat. We looked at each other for what I knew was to be the last time. Then, he put the car in drive and left me standing there. I ran out to the road, only to see the rear lights slowly fade away into the darkness. I stood there for only God knows how many minutes, waiting to see if he would return.

He never did.

I briefly flashed back to the day we met when he watched **ME** drive away. The irony was not lost on me. We had literally come full circle.

SIDEBAR: *Post-Traumatic Stress Disorder* (commonly known as "PTSD") is **not** exclusive to members of our military. There have been times I've driven past a cornfield located *nowhere near* the incident, and I instantaneously have flashbacks of that ghastly night.

The Bathroom Was My Dungeon

"My Daddy Dearest"

Alone, cold, and scared beyond belief, I walked back to the phone booth and made a call I had hoped never to make: I called my father. Through a flood of tears, I explained to him the events of the night and concluded with, *"I need a ride."* After explaining to him where I was, I had a seat on the store's step and waited for what felt like an eternity for my father's arrival.

While waiting, a police car drove past and slowed down, but the officer didn't stop to check on me. I have no doubt he (or she) saw me, though. I was seated on the steps directly under the light! *Was it common for a person to sit on the store's steps at 2:00 in the morning and not be a cause for concern?* Wow. Just...wow.

When my father finally arrived, I climbed into the car and thanked him for waking up in the middle of the night to get me. I was so ashamed. My father and I were very close. I could tell him **ANYTHING** without fear of judgment or reprimand, yet I chose to keep hidden the abuse I endured. That night, however, I told it **ALL**. He listened attentively and, when I was done, simply stated, *"You can spend the night at my house.*

In the morning, we will get this straightened out." Those words of comfort and surety allowed me to get a solid night's sleep — one free from the nightmares that had often plagued my dreams since the abuse first started.

That morning, my father had already devised a game plan: **HE** was going to call the police to report the car stolen. He also instructed me to wait until he got off work to go to my house. He didn't want anything more to happen to me and felt if he were not there to protect me, that would be my end.

Meanwhile, I contacted one of my neighbors and shared with her a brief account of the night before. I asked that she call me **immediately** should Kase return to the house with my car so that I could call the police and have him escorted away with just his clothes and personal belongings. Midday, that call came. I thanked my neighbor and called the police department's non-emergency number. After giving them the case number that was assigned to my father, the police went to my home, found my husband there, and gave him five minutes to gather some things before escorting him off the property.

For the first time in a *LONG* time, I was genuinely **JOYFUL!** I could feel the scales of the past year begin to shed.

The Bathroom Was My Dungeon

My load was lightening, and I was gearing up for the final battle. **I was READY!**

Angela R. Edwards

"Gone Up the River"

Although Kase had been removed from the home, I still wasn't comfortable with staying in the house. I am grateful that my aunt agreed to allow me to stay with her while my children stayed with their paternal grandmother right down the street during that trying time in my life.

My aunt is a fighter—literally. She was not about to allow **ANYTHING** to happen to me. She used to say, *"I WISH that mother fucker would come here! I have something waiting for him!"* I felt secure and safe in her care. I remained with her for a couple of weeks, making periodic trips back home to gather fresh clothing and checking on the house.

One day, I received another call from my neighbor. She informed me that Kase had gotten locked back up due to a parole violation. I was **ELATED!** I could finally go back home! I knew he was going to go away for a *LONG* time, which was one of his fears and why calling the police on him was a **BIG** no-no. At that news, I thanked my aunt for her hospitality and went home.

The Bathroom Was My Dungeon

"Broken Glass"

Life was finally getting back to normal for my children and me. One of the first tasks I tackled was filing with the courts to obtain an Order of Protection. Within three days of filing, I had secured a document that stated Kase was to stay away from us for the rest of our **LIVES**. I still have that order with me today.

It felt good to be free from the abuse and uncertainty that enveloped my days. I was thankful to God for His hand on my life and how He kept me sane and safe through it all. The enemy tried to take me out, **BUT GOD!**

Just as I was getting comfortable with being home alone, another horror awaited me.

While sleeping upstairs in my room one night, I was startled out of my sleep by a hand being placed over my mouth. I struggled and turned around to come face-to-face with a neighbor who had stripped butt naked and climbed into my bed. I bit his hand, causing him to release his grip. I then screamed his name and yelled, *"What the FUCK are you doing in my house?"*

He jumped up out of the bed, seemingly startled by him being recognized in the dark. He then grabbed his clothes and pleaded, *"Please don't tell anyone. I'm sorry. I don't know what I was thinking."* He then flew down the stairs and exited the way he came in—out the back door.

Once I calmed down (and my heart stopped racing), I ran downstairs to the back door. It was then I noticed he had broken out one of the nine glass panes and unlocked the door from the inside. I was **LIVID!** *What did he want? What **WAS** he thinking? Was he going to **RAPE** me? If so, what stopped him from following through?* (I know now! Angels! Heavenly angels!) How was I going to get my door fixed? Fearing his return, I remained downstairs that night with a cast iron skillet resting on my chest. I was prepared to dish out a beatdown. Thankfully, no further events occurred.

The following morning, I calmly approached him while outside and told him he needed to fix my damn door! I could tell he was ashamed of his actions because he could not look me in the face. He came over and provided a temporary fix: a piece of cardboard cut to size and duct tape to cover the broken pane. I then stressed to him that I did not appreciate whatever it was he tried to do and that he **WILL** pay to have the glass replaced. He again apologized (no explanation given) and readily agreed to my demand. Within hours, he had contacted a contractor who came and replaced the broken glass.

I often wonder what would have happened that night. I do know that man was one of those who *also* got high. *How long had he been planning on violating my space and me?* I shudder as I think about it. I chose not to tell anyone because, at the time, I was still emotionally scarred and didn't think anyone would believe me—mainly because he didn't follow through with his "plan." I had no proof other than a broken windowpane, so I kept silent.

Sometime later, after mentioning that instance to a close friend of mine, I learned that the men in his family have a **history** of sexual assault charges.

To **GOD** be the glory for me not being added to *THAT* list of victims!

Angela R. Edwards

"The Gavel Ended It All"

It was official. My marriage to Kase was over just as fast as it started. On our one-year anniversary, I was a divorcee at the tender age of 26. It was an uncontested divorce, primarily because he was still in the penitentiary at the time.

I stood before the judge with my lawyer at my side and heard the words, *"Your divorce is granted on the grounds of irreconcilable differences."* The judge slammed down the gavel, and that was it!

GLORY! GLORY! GLORY! I WAS FREE!

A month or so after the divorce was finalized, I received a letter in the mail from Kase. He **KNEW** not to call me. I didn't open the envelope for months, as I didn't want anything to do with him whatsoever. I didn't want to read his lies and fake apologies. Simply put, I wasn't ready to forgive him. The letter sat in my junk drawer for so long, I actually forgot about it until the day I needed to retrieve something else, and there it was. By that time, I was mentally in a better position to sit and read it.

The Bathroom Was My Dungeon

Just as suspected, it was everything I thought it would be. The Holy Bible says there is nothing new under the sun, and Kase tried his best to prove to me he was a new man. **NOT!** He was "new" because he was locked away and had no other choice but to be! The days of me being the fool were long gone. I didn't even finish reading the letter. I ripped it into pieces — and then put it back together with tape. I never know when I may need it.

To this day, I still have it…somewhere.

"The Lesson"

And so, life "after Kase" forged ahead, whether I was ready or not. I had to wrestle my way back to the woman I was before he and I met: strong, confident, and self-assured. That battle did not come without **MORE** mistakes made along the way, though. Sadly, other men (yes, *plural* of man) entered my life who were **also** victims of the enemy's grip of cocaine addiction.

I had to stop and ask myself, *"What is it that I am not LEARNING? What am I missing here?!"* After all, the teachings will continue until the lesson is totally comprehended, correct? That's been **MY** experience anyway.

The answer to the question about what I seemed to be missing may seem obvious to **YOU**, but as for me, when the revelation came, I felt as if I had been struck by lightning, lived to tell about it, and then got struck in the same place **AGAIN!**

Are you ready? Here it goes! My lesson was…

I CANNOT LOVE SOMEONE CLEAN!

The Bathroom Was My Dungeon

It really was that simple—and that complicated. Let me explain.

Those who **KNOW** me can attest to my nurturing nature. I desire to see the best in everyone and, to that end, **USED** to find it my life's mission to "help those who needed help the most." There's something to be said about gaining clarity. Once I "GOT IT"…once I **LEARNED** the lesson, I was able to fully awaken to my purpose—and loving someone clean wasn't "it." I had to release myself of that train of thought and sit at the feet of God to receive guidance on *"What do I do now?"*

Perhaps I had misinterpreted the passage of scripture that says, *"Above all, love each other deeply, because love covers over a multitude of sins"* (1 Peter 4:8). As many do, I confused **romantic** love with *Agape* love. Romantic love is conditional; Agape love is not and directly relates to **God's** love and how it should shape our human character.

I gave away my romantic love to men who weren't deserving. In that respect, I now consider myself a stellar student! I got it now and have since met and married a man who understands me, walks the walk with me, and encompasses the very nature of my father as a provider and protector. **FINALLY,** I feel the romantic love in return for all that I have to offer! **To GOD be the glory!**

The Bathroom Was My Dungeon

"Today, I am Battle-Scar Free!"

At the time of this writing, it has been over 20 years since that short (but tragic and life-changing) phase in my life. Every once in a blue moon, something will happen that triggers memories of that period. The hairs will rise on my neck and arms as if I were living in that moment all over again. I have to remind myself that I am no longer subjected to that abuse. I am **FREE** from the dungeon. I could have had the support and help early on in my "situation," but because of shame, I kept it hidden from those who love and genuinely care for me.

The healing journey hasn't been easy, but I did it—and you can, too! As one who believes in the power of words, the very telling of my story here is a significant part of that healing process all these years later.

I cannot fail to acknowledge the first time I publicly shared just a *portion* of my survivor story. I am grateful to God and Dr. Marilyn Porter's "Motivationally ME" ("MOME") Facebook platform for the speaking opportunity that led to my breakthrough. During one of Dr. Porter's MOME Women's Ministry teleconferences, I was a guest speaker. The night I told my story, my now-grown daughter was on the call. She and the other attendees listened attentively as I poured out my soul. When I was done, Dr. Porter asked if there were any comments. A few women spoke and offered words of encouragement and praise for my strength. Shortly after the last woman finished, my daughter's voice came on the line. She was crying hysterically when she said, *"Mommy, I never knew. You are so strong! Thank you for keeping it from me. I don't know what I would've done to him had I known."* At the time, my daughter and granddaughter were living with me. After the call ended, I ran into her room, embraced her, and begged that she **NEVER** allow a man to subject her to the abuse I had endured.

Victims of abuse often compartmentalize tragedy. I have no doubt there are things stored away in the recesses of my mind that refuse to come to the forefront. I have decided not to dive in to retrieve them. I've endured enough horror to last me a lifetime and desire not to give voice to those things that choose to remain in hiding. No longer will I slap myself in the forehead while asking, *"What was I **THINKING**?!"* Instead, I opt for the high road and ask, *"What did I **LEARN**?"* The latter is a much kinder question, wouldn't you agree?

What I have penned here is a story that will likely resonate with many. It is my sincere prayer that whatever is for you has been shared in such a way that you know you, too, **WILL** survive. You *MUST!* There's a testimony waiting to be told that **ONLY YOU** can tell.

Conversely, if my story is not your story, you are encouraged to share it with another — be it woman or man. After all, men are victims of abuse, too — although not talked about often enough.

There are always two sides to every story. What's been shared with you is clearly my one-sided experience and viewpoint. I am sure if Kase were to tell his story, it would be remarkably different. Should he ever rise to the occasion and pen his tale, it would be interesting to gain insight into his world…his thoughts…his "why." I truly do not wish my abuser any ill will. As stated before, I try to see the good in everyone. Do I feel a tug to see him ever again? **NOPE.** Do I forgive him? I have done just that a *LONG* time ago. I **HAD** to forgive because it was a part of my healing process and because God's Word directs us to forgive others as **HE** has forgiven us.

We all have the power of *choice*. Even when a narcissistic abuser works diligently to eradicate your control, always know there is an alternative decision to be made that **ONLY YOU** can make. You may be beaten down. You may feel that all hope is lost. You may even feel suicidal. When you find yourself at the end of your rope, utter these two words:

BUT GOD!

He will hear you! Put your faith to work. Believe that *GOD* has better in store for you and that whatever you're enduring will prove to be a **POWERFUL** testament of His grace and glory over your life. Believe it! Receive it!

Before I go, I must take a moment to give a special acknowledgment to my mother, Mrs. Marlowe R. Scott. She will likely read this book from cover to cover and learn some things she didn't know about my turbulent marriage to Kase. I pray she understands **ALL** that I endured *had* to happen. As one of my biggest supporters and cheerleaders in everything I do, I am saddened at the very thought that she may be disappointed in me; however, I want her *AND* you to know what I went through was **NOT** because of her lack of parenting, mistreatment, or anything else. No matter my decisions, she always supported them and allowed me to make my mistakes so that I could learn from them. I am forever grateful to my mom for the love and support she has always given me — despite **MY** life's choices. Thank you, Mommy! I love you!

And so, my story continues, but no longer am I bound by the chains of abuse. The level of freedom I am experiencing today is beyond phenomenal! I am no longer a victim; I am a **SURVIVOR** and **THRIVER!**

I AM BATTLE-SCAR FREE!

*It takes strength to endure abuse.
It takes courage to stop it.*

****

I am who I am because the tears of my past have watered the magnificence of my present.

Pen Your Pain: The Healing Begins

On the pages that follow, you are encouraged to journal your way to healing. With each stroke of the pen, release those things that the enemy has lied to you about and told you would keep you bound in anguish for your lifetime. Take your time. Reflect on the painful truths shared in this book. It took some **DELIBERATE** "doing" to reach the level of peace I now have. I desire and pray the same for you.

Give voice to your pain. Let the healing begin!

Angela R. Edwards

The Bathroom Was My Dungeon

The Bathroom Was My Dungeon

Angela R. Edwards

The Bathroom Was My Dungeon

Angela R. Edwards

About the Author

Angela R. Edwards is the CEO and Chief Editorial Director of Pearly Gates Publishing, LLC (PGP) and Redemption's Story Publishing, LLC (RSP) — Award-Winning International Christian Book Publishing Houses located in Houston, Texas. In May 2018, PGP was honored as the 2018 Winner of Distinction for Publishing in South Houston, Texas, by the Better Business Bureau (BBB). In 2018 and 2019, she was awarded BBB Gold Star Certificates for both entities for her exemplary service to the community.

Angela R. Edwards

Angela's mantra is *"My Words Have POWER!"* Since its inception in January 2015, PGP has been blessed with an ever-growing and diverse group of almost 100 authors who have penned topics related to faith, love, abuse, bullying, Bible study tools, marriage, and so much more. Their youngest author is only three years old; their eldest is 75 years old at the time of this publication. To their credit and God's glory, PGP and RSP collectively have over 150 best-selling titles to date.

An affordable publishing option (in comparison to some of the large, traditional publishing houses), PGP and RSP work one-on-one with authors to ensure that financial hardship is not a discouraging part of the publishing process. For those desiring to share their God-inspired messages for the masses, to include both new and 'seasoned' authors, both publishing houses provide unique services and support that many have said "left them feeling as if they are the only author" placed under each company's care.

The Holy Bible states that *"God loves a cheerful giver"* (2 Corinthians 9:7). To that end, PGP and RSP are frequently found hosting fantastic giveaways. Throughout the past few years, new author contests have awarded authors over $14,000.00 in products and services total.

In addition to the aforementioned, Angela is a domestic abuse survivor. Since first telling her abuse-survivor story publicly, she has become a 'Trumpet for Change.' She established the **"Battle-Scar Free Movement"** — an online community of individuals who freely express and share their own overcoming-testimonies while, at the same time, begin the vital healing process of the heart, mind, and soul. As part of her God-given mission, she provides abuse victims and survivors a **FREE** opportunity to anonymously share their testimonies in a book series entitled *God Says I am Battle-Scar Free*. Although the series will be completed in the Spring of 2021, Angela's mission to help individuals heal with the power of their words will continue. Assisting others with the healing process is paramount to her, which propelled her into becoming a volunteer Mentor for the Star of Hope Mission in Houston, Texas.

Angela holds an A.A. Degree in Business Administration from the University of Phoenix and is working towards her B.S. Degree in Psychology with a concentration in Christian Counseling from LeTourneau University. She is a woman of God, wife, mother, grandmother of 12, daughter, sister, and trusted friend. Originally a New Jersey native, she has since made Texas her home and embraced the southern culture in all its fullness. She loves life and affirms daily: **"NOT TODAY, SATAN!"**

Contact the Publisher

Redemption's Story Publishing is always looking for new talent and desires to "birth the writer" in **YOU**! Will *YOU* be next on their list of Best-Selling Authors?

Contact us today!

Visit RSP on the Web at www.Redemptions-Story.com

Connect with RSP on Facebook at
www.facebook.com/RedemptionsStoryPublishing

Email Angela Edwards, CEO at
RedeemedByHim@Redemptions-Story.com

Call 1-832-994-8797
to schedule your **FREE** 15-minute publishing consultation.

Angela R. Edwards